DREAM OF THE LAKE

DREAM

OF THE

LAKE

POEMS

CAROLINE M. MAR

DURHAM, NORTH CAROLINA

Dream of the Lake

Copyright ©2022 by Caroline M. Mar

Library of Congress Cataloging-in-Publication Data

Names: Mar, Caroline M., 1983- author.
Title: Dream of the lake : poems / Caroline M. Mar.
Description: Durham, North Carolina : Bull City Press, [2022]
Identifiers: LCCN 2021063105 | ISBN 9781949344318 (paperback)
Subjects: LCGFT: Poetry.
Classification: LCC PS3613.A68 D74 2022 | DDC 811/.6--dc23/eng/20220107
LC record available at https://lccn.loc.gov/2021063105

Published in the United States of America

Cover concept: Quinton Okoro
Cover artwork: "Knot" by Blondinrikard Fröberg
Image: *bit.ly/3FMA43y* License (CC-BY): *bit.ly/3pOxWTz*
Author photo: Jessica Tong-Ahn
Book design: Spock and Associates

Published by BULL CITY PRESS
1217 Odyssey Drive
Durham, NC 27713
www.BullCityPress.com

CONTENTS

. . . at last the Lake burst upon us—a noble sheet of blue water lifted six thousand three hundred feet above the level of the sea, and walled in by a rim of snow-clad mountain peaks that towered aloft full three thousand feet higher still!
. . . As it lay there with the shadows of the mountains brilliantly photographed upon its still surface I thought it must surely be the fairest picture the whole earth affords.

—Mark Twain describing Lake Tahoe, *Roughing It*

The precise number of Chinese who worked on the railroad from 1864 to 1869 is not clear; records are incomplete and inexact. . . . Historians estimate that at any one time as many as 10,000 to 15,000 Chinese were working on constructing the railroad. Most Chinese probably did not work for the entire duration of construction and others would take their place, particularly because the work was so difficult and dangerous.

—*Chinese Railroad Workers in North America Project*, Stanford University

遺 産

Where can I set this inheritance down?
Maybe every winter was like this, once.

    I know every winter was like this once,
    the whiteness devised to draw us in.

The ways whiteness devises to draw us in:
We will not hurt you. A gentle approach.

    It won't hurt you; take the gentlest approach:
    a rustic wood bench, a sheepskin throw pillow.

Rustic wood benches, sheepskin throw pillows;
who needs a fence when the bears walk through?

    No need for a fence. The bears walk through,
    always hungry. They do so much needing.

I am always hungry, full of my needing.
I know how to spend an inheritance down.

STAGE 1: COLD SHOCK

THREAT NO. 1 LOSS OF BREATHING CONTROL

Gasping

There are an average of seven drownings per year in the lake, most due
to cold water shock, even among those who are capable swimmers. Or were
before the water folded them into itself:

a pocket of failure, a slipped
seam of darkness out of the summer
sun's light.

Hyperventilation

My body in the summer heat, skin a prickling of sweat, the stick
of flesh to seat before I rise, look out over the edge, and dive.

My lungs seizing together inside my chest: a cavity curling inward.
The body, built for survival. The water still icy from snowmelt.

Difficulty holding your breath

It takes a certain force to move your limbs
     as you tread water. Remember to cup your hands,
like this. To kick just so, and steady.
     To keep your neck above the waves, to gulp air
like guilt, to hold it before you let it go.

Feeling of suffocation

I have felt this shock in my own body. The delicate line
between body and brain. The pain
of doing the thing that keeps you alive.

STAGE 1: COLD SHOCK

THREAT NO. 2 HEART AND BLOOD PRESSURE PROBLEMS

Cold water immersion causes my body to shudder, to shock,
an instantaneous and massive exuberance and joy,
increase in heart rate and blood pressure because there is racing doubt, possibility of failure,
all the blood vessels in your skin might explode, or might survive, might
constrict in response to the body? A live wire, electric, dangerous, it is
sudden cooling, which is far more intense against the water's conductivity, deeper
in water than in air. In vulnerable cells, the cold awakens something,
individuals, this greatly increases my certainty that my life has meaning.
the danger of heart silly heart, hopeful heart, busted heart, swim through
failure and stroke.

STAGE 1: COLD SHOCK

THREAT NO. 3 MENTAL PROBLEMS

aquaphobia: fear of water, specifically of drowning

claustrophobia: fear of suffocation and restriction

hydrophobia: fear of water

   though the human body is 80% water

ichthyophobia: fear of fish

      that time we ate lobster on a beach in Cuba and you laughed and laughed, delighted

      that your fear had subsided, you no longer believed

      it was swimming around inside you

xenophobia: fear of the unknown

chromophobia: fear of a color

   in this case, I suppose the color

   would be blue

achluophobia, or nyctophobia, or scotophobia, or lygophobia: fear of darkness

   most children have this, it is not abnormal

   to fear the loss of a sense, sight being

   one upon which we rely heavily to understand what is happening

   around us, just look

   how many names, though none

   are clinical

thanatophobia: fear of dying

phobophobia: fear of fear

   : fear of not being found

         those rumors, again—

         all those bodies

   : fear of being found

   : fear of being too late

STAGE 2: PHYSICAL INCAPACITATION

When the waters rose, the forest stayed. What else can a forest do
but stand. There would be no fire inside the lake.

There would be no ground to tumble down. Just water rising,
cold and blue, the floods of the next era.

Sometimes the change comes over you like that all at once. A drowning.

Hundreds of coolies were tied together and weighed down
with rocks. Straw hats removed, queues tangled, bodies thrown in to save

the cost of their pay. The historians say this is unlikely. Given
the railroad payrolls showing each Chinese contractor paid,

given how little Chinese labor cost, given the distance
from the Truckee railroad camp to the lake. Given

every other history I know:
chains, bodies of water, ghosts—

Sometimes a person isn't a person at all, but a weight
to be freighted onto someone else's shoulder.

Why not the silent lake? Why not a flood of furious bodies
fighting toward the coldest surface?

The forest stayed, and drowned.

STAGE 3: HYPOTHERMIA

The lake is steel-shirred gray, a sheet of velvet,
soft-napped. Water barely stirring. The snow
is loud as an earthquake, house shaking

with dropped weight as the slide overcomes
the roofline. Winter's thundering reminder:
some things cannot be stopped.

The snow is loud beneath the plow, its spray
an arc of meditation. The snow clings, a sticky sheet,
to the sides of the sweating trees. This cannot last

forever. Snow melts into the lake, the icy rocks.
Winter: gray and gray and gray; crystalline
whiteness. The graydark water will not freeze,

the lake too deep. And what can survive
that kind of cold? *Nothing, nothing,* my mind's
lie: the fish are fattening, swimming slow.

Yes, too, the snow is quiet. Muffling every sound
but the crunch of my footfalls following
the shape of your boot prints, as I follow you.

STAGE 4: CIRCUM-RESCUE COLLAPSE

an erasure

                         can happen just before   The symp-
toms   faint   . But, why

                                 fight   to stay alive,

survive. Once   a mental
relaxation occurs
            can drop   can fail
               .   remember   heart   is
                                            the
water. Knowing   a   difference.

             it is this

                  the greatest   survival. Some
of these actions might even seem counter-intuitive
          ,   understand
        .

DREAM OF THE LAKE

You are not the sea, but I confuse you
with the sea, awash in the blood
beneath my skin

> What are the sailor's tools
> What burns me to the touch

Slip knot
Bowline knot
> *Better to know a knot*

On your surface, my skin darkens
all summer, bloodbrown
like a tree's rough bark

> My unanswered questions
> uprooted and sky-turned

Clove hitch
Sheet bend
> *and not need it*

Here: let me anchor you
I can't say blood blooms, as if
it weren't the other way around

> I'm no fish,
> you're no ocean

Rolling hitch
Stopper knot
> *than to need a knot*

I see you looking at me, my blood
gutters, gathering
like baubles off a broken string

                    I an unspooled skein,
                    a daughter unmoored

        and not know it

MYTHOLOGY

The partial truths: That the water preserves. That the water
　　　is so cold it slows bacterial action. What is false: That the water
keeps whole, that there are no fish to nibble the morsels
　　　of cheek and jowl, the curl of an eyelid. That the water is clear
to a depth of one hundred feet. In fact, it is clear to a depth
　　　of sixty-nine. At least, this was true at last measure, a disk in the water,
a wavering white eye seen until it sputters closed, though
　　　it depends upon weather, season, and algae content within the water.
That there are hundreds, held down deep, eyes open, seeking
　　　the shoreline's rocky light, empty sockets and insolent grins.
That there is a creature, maybe beastly, maybe beautiful,
　　　cruising her slow sweet way through the watery canyons
of glacier-carved granite. That there is a tunnel connecting elsewhere,
　　　that this is what allows bodies drowned here to finally float up
in some other lake. That there are mysteries we cannot solve
　　　deep beneath this surface, in that darkness below seventy feet.
That we cannot know. That what we do not know,
　　　we imagine, we retell. That the water's whispers are worth retelling.

INTELLIGIBLE

My name a rearing horse, curved into
its evolution. Logographic,

four legs like drops of sweat falling
from a shaking body.

The etymological—or is it orthographical—
origin of the word *clear* is the word *blue-green*.

Radical : water : drops from a brush
on a page, swishing into newness, so

becoming : the clarity we use for death.
Semantic-phonetic, each stroke's symbiosis

of sound and meaning. A morpheme
rather than a phoneme. Clear morning,

we greet our dead and deathly, send gifts
for the moving-on. Not darkness, nor night :

our dead aren't afraid of the day's blue face.
May our dead float back to this thin surface, deep

blue to bluegreen to clear. I see the way the light
moves through the water. The way the light moves

through. What is it you do to honor your dead
in the after? In an account I read, you burn them,

too. We all need something to carry
into the next world. Its watery edge. I know

what I said : I don't believe in any next thing.
Yet I see ghosts, see memory. Look how I am

haunted. The smoke like a clot in my lung.
Shh, shh, drink now. The water is cool.

Rinse the ash from your face.

SONG FOR GREAT-GRANDFATHER

Your son's spindly fingers are mine, made me good at piano, means my fingers are yours, maybe the forehead, too, though I didn't get the ears, blooming like cliff woodbeauties. Lucky girl. My fingers can reach beyond a full octave. Keys merganser-dark, gull-white. Lanky, a pickaxe in your hand, the arm's sinuous extension, a flow like the water you must have known how to swim in. Your body turning, smooth, as we float in the water. The water is clear-cold, as always. It hurts when I open my eyes in the sunlight. A few brown trees among the green, the rocks dark-wet underwater like the backs of whales. Above the water line, the sun glitters off the mica in the granite. Glitters off the water like day-stars. Still, I see you: your arm-swing sliding up and down the scale of the rocks.

calls me forth, earthbound
each solid ring a note
someday, somewhere: song

TRAGEDY

One of the Chinese had been skewered by an iron brake rod and was screaming for somebody to shoot him.

—E. B. Scott, *The Saga of Lake Tahoe*

I think of the white man who lived after an iron rod—
also from the railroad, also a brake rod, perhaps—
speared him right through his brain. Medical marvel.
The conflicting accounts of whether or not the injury
caused personality change. Early neurology, psychology:
his daguerreotype affixed in the gilt-framed textbooks
of our memory. It is unclear whether [the Chinese] was,
or was not, shot. Whether he survived, was too a marvel
with a hole in his gut, or was it—no, had to be gut. To
skewer is to be food, gutted. The screaming implies not
lungs, nor throat. And the heart, well: death already. I
have screamed for somebody to let me die, but no one
had a gun. I was asking not to be saved. Oh, girlchild
sadness, epigenetic thread, disappointment stitched to
every story. In a different book, I read that [the Chinese]
had gunpowder hundreds of years before we put it to
guns. The Maya with wheels: the author's comparison.
When a tool's not worth the change it wrings. All
fireworks, no grenades; firecrackers without the
cracking of bullet. Just crush of knuckle to bone, iron to
rib. What interested the teller in this story was not the
story's inevitable end: a body, dead one way or another.
Bones shipped home for burial. A pallet box, or my
father coming home through customs: What you got in
that suitcase, son? My grandmother, he chuckles with
each retelling. We visit her every year, one of six names

on a stone. The index, too, lists six mentions of [the Chinese] in 468 pages. *Caroline* is the name of a boat, one of 162 indexed. Home is where your living will honor you, as long as they remember you: a mean old woman. A skewering tongue in my father's childhood: bitterness. Either way, I know the man in the story is dead. Crawl of infection, loss of blood, shouting recoil of mercy: somebody's. It's been too long for a miracle. The water is meant for the rush of the hull. It doesn't count each dive. 144 years, waiting for someone to call his name.

NAMING

Blank sky: too simple. You are window-streaked, edged in god's-eye white. I can see
where you took a breath, where you repeated yourself. Tiny flecks of your own voice, deepening.
Clear as an eyedrop. Settled as a vintage tear. Nothing harried about you, tiny fingers
licking your own edges. You could be a flag, flutter in anticipation of your own Wellfleet wedding.
Something old, something borrowed, a rusty earring back cast aside. You are summer's
generosity, watermelon's thinnest rind, your firework tongue in my shellshine mouth.
The antique ocean blooms, watches.

長衫

Mamah had this gaudy one: silk
the color of this water's shallowest edges
meant to be sky

& on that sky flew two gold bodies
dragon, phoenix: each finely stitched
in golden thread or thread

made gold-like by the weaving
of some kind of shimmering filament
a complicated overlap

of red and orange
of stitch and sparkle
& it did shine

The sun spiked itself out at the center
between those undulating beasts
fire-breathing and fire-born

& by center I mean I remember
the sun sat somewhere above
my navel when I put the dress on

when I spun in my certainty
I would grow up
& be beautiful: beautiful

Lay on the shine, coat me
like some dress that shows
exactly how much

the cost   & look
I've become this
for you

CERTAINTY

you know cliff diving to be dangerous and yet here you are granite beneath your feet ready for anything if you could be ready as you can be in this life you're never really ready you think you've heard you've called for a hovering leap a bound above the water so clear you can see the bottom so clear and wouldn't you like that kind of clarity about everything is this what it is that calls you to this water it is both clear and unknowable you can be certain you feel both clear and unknowable you can see the bottom you can know no rocks are hiding you know this slip is safe to return to every time this ship this little boat will stay afloat keep this water spray across your body keep this wind chopping at your face this ship that is your body will keep sailing across this water will accept the weight of you

BEING AWAY FROM THE LAKE

that thing about a tree
and a forest and falling
no one to hear

but isn't there always at least one
body one eye one ear
to witness I was far away

in a cloud forest a tree did fall
it thundered down heavy
with rain and the howler monkeys

did what they are named to do
wasn't it Eve who named
every creature

alouatta, alouatta palliata
I don't know my Bible
stories I missed that boat

that heavy load that blesséd
water on my forehead
the lake is sacred

to some maybe even
to me when I am there
it renders me

a blue and borrowed thing the water the way
it slips through one's fingers even
if you press them tight

水 客

the water a guest inside of us
salty-sweet and swimming
how water does   and you
a guest in your own house
a watery word
a guest on the tongue
a gust of air across wet lips   a voice
echoing back and back
though nothing's left to prove it no
papers no shred of evidence not one
letter not one mark upon the page
no papers
no papers
your papers
for a period of three long years
an ocean away from where you are not
a guest   where are you from
people ask me   ask people who look
like me   look like anything but
the blankness of a page
let me turn then to the color
of water into ink ground against a stone
the words carried back by each water guest
each bringer of news and love and tribulation here
are the words that belong to you
here are the words that belong

高 祖 父: A CORRESPONDENCE   :太 爺

I have no one left to ask, here
so I write to ask you these things.

Did you ever see this lake? Were you one
of those who scaled that nearby pass?
As you looked across this gorgeous landscape, all
granite all tallpine all blueair, tell me
what you thought—

I am certain you could write, would write,
would have written. And so someone read your letters
to your blinded son, and so he would recite later
all that he had learned because blindness
doesn't bind memory.

Did you mistake the moraine's slide, glacier-carved
like the face of your forgotten daughter,
for struggle?

Did you hate the mountains for the work—
armswing pickswing hammerswing shovelswing—
they wrung out of you?

                    Though I am not certain you could write,
                      would write, would have written, maybe
                        you did. That someone would have read
                    your letters to your barely literate son, that
                          he might know your voice in his ear.

When you were here, did the woods still smell
of baked rock, crumbled sugar pine? Or had the silt
and gilt timber barons already tumbled it all down
to the water's murk-washed edge?

清 明: we burn you papers, incense, oranges
in a pile. Flowers and flowers mounded upon each grave.

The ghosts of those who died in these mountains
are doomed forever. The One-Eyed Wanderer,

exploded to just a hand. Old Three-Moles, washed
away in a dam burst. Squeakylaugh impaled on a rail.

Longteeth. Shitforbrains. Short Chung and Fat Chung,
both. No body means nobody to bury, no body

to call home. No one to tell them
hit the road, cross over, cross over—

Would it be so bad if these mountains were your
eternity? The thinner air of heaven.

The mountains are calling and I must go.

The blue like a lance to your heart.

Blue the basin the basket the berry the juice blue that counters the yellow of
bleach bluing blue indigo blue dye #4 blue the bruise the bitter blue anything
but an eye please blue the water the wash the vein in my body the vein in my
earth our earth the sapphire blue the glittering dark sky at night sky at day sky
at blue note sounding blue the print the plan the next step into blue the brazen
the bold the navy the few the proud who wants that blues sing it again sister
bluer than blue my blue blood true blood tv fantasy blue light blue screen blue

movie blue balls blue butch blue black battered and beaten or blue like a piece
of glass with the sun shining through it blue as a shard a shatter a splatter of
water blue blur that won't leave me don't sparkle for just anything don't break

My father loves to tell your departure:
how you crashed from the open window into the garden
to escape your brother's swinging sword, how this was what drove you
to ship, to sea, to foreign shore.

How in your body's absence,
your brother blinded your baby for spite.
Your eyes turned toward the track's next turn.

Heaven could be the smell of pines
and snowmelt under your boots.

Heaven could be the color of this water
at precisely twenty-two feet deep.

My father wrote his father's story, how first your brother
and later he, your eldest son, departed to cover
your foolish debts. Your rescue from debtor's prison.
But there was, too, a before, though your son never told him
what it was like when you yourself were away
making some kind of living in 金 山.

What I don't know:

The blast of dynamite.
The whistle of engine.

Dreams of railroad spikes falling
from your son's eyes.

Am I mistaken, calling this place *beauty*. Nothing
but leisure-seeking on the lake's cool skin.
Unperturbed, the water slips into
my mouth whenever I swim.

who tutored your son to memorize the texts
he must have later used to teach his students
what was done to his mother in your absence
if she was your only wife, her name, the names
of your son's wives who were not my great-
grandmother, the names of his nonsurviving
children who were my great aunts and uncles,
whether he was gentle or harsh with them,
the names of your nonsurviving children, of any
of the servants, who it was you loved, if anyone,
if you wanted to kill your brother, too, and why
you didn't, what it was like when you returned

what happened to your brother when he returned,
what happened to you in debtor's prison, what was done
to your wife in your absence, or the two before her,
their names, the names of your nonsurviving children
— and —, the names of her sisters, her mother, her
friends, whether you were gentle or harsh, if it was you
who taught my grandfather not to use his hands
on children, who it was you loved, if anyone, if you wanted
to stay or to leave, what it was like when you returned

I understand why you don't answer.

I know the answers. There are
no answers. I am the only
possible outcome here.

Let's not pretend you would have cared
what happened to me except I am
your dream of 金 山 made real—

My rings: of gold. My dress: of gold.
My eyes: of gold. My skin: of gold.
My mouth: my mouth: my mouth.

Of late—no, since I was a child—
I've spent a lot of time wondering
about the *bachelor society.*

What secrecy that invites: all those bodies,
men and male, kept close
in their togetherness.

I read only silence.

Did a 水 客 carry your letters for you? I, too,
would be a guest in your house, a guest
made of water, a guest in every house
on this land that shouldn't belong to me.

Golden goddess of good luck, god
of glory and gory success, shine of someone's
fortune, scent of dragon scale and slippery
glinting teeth: you chase and chase it.

What song survives
the work you did, the stories you told

your blind son waiting for your return

                    your mute son waiting for your return

      your daughters lost to history like your letters

When you died did you hear
music? Was it the clinking tone
of iron into fresh-laid track?

I can make you whoever
I need you to be, but I can't stop
asking you these questions.

Tell me, how did you die?

It was you who died in the street:
your old head unbent and unbowed
before a soldier's rifle butt.

What is your relationship
to color? Does 藍 even begin
to cover it? Is 金 a color?
I know no nuance in this
unsimplified tongue.

水, 金: two words I still remember.

When I say 茶, your

great-   granddaughter

mocks my singing accent, lilt
of my gold-laden tongue
against your language's watery shore.

Tiger balm smell of 嫲 嫲's sore knees.
I imagine your knees after each day's labor.

Your shoulders' ache. Each body's work takes
a different weight. Who was the one who rubbed
the knots, who laid a sweet and gentle palm—
though rough, like yours—
against your tender hurts?

Tell me about him, who
loved you best. Who you hid,
who hid you.

your lips

Was it
to
pressed in those claustrophobic
kindling rooms?

your lips,

In Hong Kong, I was shy to speak
to the other women. *I have a girlfriend,*
too, finally, then laughter. A culture
of women away from family and homeland,
awash in women's work and the ways
it buckled them, but still: a kind of relief.

You're teaching me the beauty
of revisionist history. I make you lovers
because, yes, it is in my power, because
my ancestral altar needs a queerer root.
Because, too, I am afraid of the smoke-
thick danger of you if you were not:

girl children in locked cages—

who could love a man like that?

How quick the language slips
from our gold-plated tongues.

I have been keeping secrets
from the woman I love.

Here's what I remember:
我 愛 你 。紅 。海 。
東 南 西 北 。

I remember my name, part
of my father's and his father's.
I never knew

yours.   yours.

I should have asked your granddaughter
when I had the chance. I should have
known your name.

                                        I should have asked your son
                                when I had the chance. I should have
                                                known your name.

Tell me about your mistakes,
what they cost you. Blood
on your palm, or tears in your mouth.
So like sweat on the tongue.

I am sure this was not your dream.

I was not your dream.

The kindling rooms: every plank a match unstruck,
a burn waiting to consume. Every Chinatown
burned down more than once.

Picturing you driven out: a stick against
your strong back, a frothing white face
spitting rage race and fear. Or maybe
you were one of those who went out,
bought a rifle or two, armed in the way
of your temporary homeland.

I'm not sure our hands aren't bloody.
I am losing track of each detail
I have forgotten, like the wood inlay
chipping slowly out of my 箱.

Maybe it's your blood I feel tingling
when I turn my own gun in my palm.
We know what it is to defend ourselves.

I like the smell of my own skin
after sun, and the smell of pine
pitch and pollen. Is this vanity?

This story may have gotten away from us.
Your life unravels

off my unruly hand.

I do not understand why you don't answer.

I think I am telling the wrong story. I think
I care more about your wife, your wives, your
long-dead daughters.

When you raise a daughter,
you are raising someone else's slave.

Don't they still belong to me?

I could decide to make you happy.

Gold is the eye the tongue the lion
Gold the mountain the valley the river gold
the nugget the ingot the flake the flume
the fairy the dust the feather the fatherland
Gold the sun and the sunlight the son
You wanted sons and sons and sons
Gold the daughter in spite of gold
the bangles and bracelets and rings
Gold the ornate and elaborate
Hold me, here: this is my ordinary hand

Because *only barbarians touch like that*

I am free to build you in my own image.

Your mouth on another man's mouth
unafraid or maybe afraid, quiet
in a boardinghouse bed or a canvas tent
the hurried rush of your bodies
before shift change or exhaustion or
the call to supper. The joy of it.

I'd rather not be gold-dusted, shimmer
of bronzers and glimmering lotions, potions
of nanoparticles that never break down
and will float forever in this water, in the gut
of a fish, in my blood. No.

I'd rather think about blue.

The waves tick the clock of my patience.
Each pine a pictogram of response:
here, a word on your gratitude; here,
a word on your hunger.

I turn and turn the page but no more story comes.
You were here, I think,
perhaps stood where I stood.

You believed in shamans, oracles,
fortune tellers, other small gods.
What they told you about this future:

could you see me on this shore? A rock
in my palm, the shape
of an opened mouth.

You died   You died

seven thousand miles away.
The water is different water.
The trees are different trees.

How long the journey. How long
your death-blunted life. How long until I knew

even enough of our story
to know it wasn't enough.

I'm waiting for your echo to call back
across the smallest waves.

Swim, swim for the caves with me, let's find
the rock where our voices come singing.
Tell me how you survived winter.

Tell me about blue, about how you shouted
and shuddered when your feet touched the water
each time you bathed in the cold spring air.

NOTES & ACKNOWLEDGMENTS

"Dream of the Lake"

    The italicized text is an old sailor's saying.

"Stage 1: Cold Shock / Threat No. 1 Loss of Breathing Control" and "Threat No. 2 Heart and Blood Pressure Problems"

    The italicized text in both poems is from the National Center for Cold Water Safety's web page on cold shock. The titles of both poems, and of the following three poems, are also from this website: www.coldwatersafety.org/ColdShock.html.

"Stage 4: Circum-rescue Collapse"

    The original text was taken from the online article "4 Phases of Cold Water Immersion," *Beyond Cold Water Bootcamp*. beyondcoldwaterbootcamp.com/4-phases-of-cold-water-immersion#Circum-rescue%20Collapse.

"高祖父 : A Correspondence : 太爺"

    "The mountains are calling. . ." is a quote from John Muir. "When you raise a daughter. . ." is something I remember being attributed as a common Chinese saying by Pearl S. Buck in *The Good Earth*, but I haven't bothered to fact-check that memory because I don't want to reread the book. During early exposure to white folks, Chinese people commonly called white people barbarians, and were disgusted by their public displays of affection.

Gratitude, gratitude, gratitude:

These journals, for first publishing some of the poems in this collection—

> *Anomaly*: "Stage 1: Cold Shock / Threat No. 1: Loss of Breathing Control," "Stage 1: Cold Shock / Threat No. 2: Heart and Blood Pressure Problems," "Stage 1: Cold Shock / Threat No. 3: Mental Problems," "Stage 2: Physical Incapacitation," "Stage 3: Hypothermia," and "Stage 4: Circum-rescue Collapse"

> *Bridges*: "Dream of the Lake" and "Naming"

> *CALYX*: "水 客"

> *Eastwind Ezine*: an excerpt of "高 祖 父 : A Correspondence : 太 爺"

> *JuxtaProse*: "Song for Great-Grandfather"

> *Indiana Review*: an excerpt of "高 祖 父 : A Correspondence : 太 爺"

> *Nimrod International Journal*: "Certainty," "Mythology," and "Tragedy"

> *Pinwheel*: "遺 產"

> *Queer Rain*: "長 衫"

Somayeh Shams, Adrienne G. Perry, Francine Conley, and Rachel Brownson, there from the very first draft.

Gordon Chang, for lunch, sources, inspiration, and the beautiful artifact that is *Ghosts of Gold Mountain: The Epic Story of the Chinese Who Built the Transcontinental Railroad*. In my life, your timing was perfect.

Eddie Wong, for being an early believer in these poems, and for giving me the first public venue to share them with an audience.

My family, born and chosen, for your endless support: Susan McDonough and Warren Mar, Sandy Metivier, Tioundra Body, Melissa Millan, Krissa Lagos, Emma Olson, Steven Noble, and the entire boisterous Mar family.

My ancestors, remembered and forgotten, haunting and at rest, better and worse than I have imagined you. 多 謝 世。

The Washoe Tribe of Nevada and California, indigenous people of the Lake Tahoe basin, for your perseverance and protection of your ancestral lands, and for sharing some of your stories with me. Special gratitude for your collaboration, guidance, and patience to the Washoe Cultural Resources Advisory Council: Darrel Cruz, Jo Ann Nevers, Dorothy McCloud, Lana Hicks, Floyd Wade, and especially Melba Rakow.

The Chinese Railroad Workers Descendants Association for planning and hosting the 2019 Golden Spike Conference in Salt Lake City, and to all the historians, filmmakers, and authors who shared their knowledge there.

The faculty and staff of the Chinese Immersion Program at West Portal Elementary from 1989 to 1995. The language and history you taught me may not have survived intact, but you gave me the tools to imagine my way back.

The Vermont Studio Center and Ragdale Foundation, for a total of three residencies where these poems were begun, worked on, and finally pulled together as a manuscript. My Ragdale Coven, for your magic: Nick White, L. Lamar Wilson, Shereen Marisol Meraji, Camellia Grass, Rage Hezekiah, Marcia Bradley, Deke Weaver, A. Martine Whitehead, Adrienne Dawes, and Dianna Frid.

Ross White and Noah Stetzer at Bull City Press for giving this book an earthly form, and you, reader, for holding it.

ABOUT THE AUTHOR

Caroline M. Mar is the great-granddaughter of a railroad laborer and the author of *Special Education* (Texas Review Press, 2020). A high school health educator in San Francisco, she is doing her best to keep her gentrified hometown queer and creative. Carrie is a graduate of the MFA Program for Writers at Warren Wilson College, an alumna of VONA, and a member of Rabble Collective. She has been granted residencies at Vermont Studio Center, Storyknife, and Ragdale.

This book was published with assistance from the Fall 2021 Editing and Publishing class at the University of North Carolina at Chapel Hill. Contributing editors and designers were alex benedict and Quinton Okoro.